Merry
Christmas
Hailey Jane !

Love,
Your Pamba

HORSE RULES

Editor/Design: Andrea Donner

Printed in Canada

Photo Credits: page 5, 6 © Denver Bryan / denverbryan.com; page 7 © Daniel Johnson; page 8, 9, 11, 12 © Dusty L. Perin; page 13 © Paulette Johnson; page 14 © Daniel Johnson; page 15 © Norvia Behling; page 17, 18, 19, 21, 22, 23, 25 © Bob Langrish; page 26 © Denver Bryan / denverbryan.com; page 27, 29, 30 © Bob Langrish; page 31 © Dusty L. Perin; page 33 © Denver Bryan / denverbryan.com; page 34, 35 © Dusty L. Perin; page 36, 37 © Denver Bryan / denverbryan.com; page 39 © Daniel Johnson; page 40 © Art Wolfe / artwolfe.com; page 41 © Dusty L. Perin; page 42 © www.ronkimballstock.com; page 43 © Bob Langrish; page 45, 46, 47 © Ron Kimball / www.ronkimballstock.com; page 49 © Bob Langrish; page 50 © Dusty L. Perin; page 51 © Ron Kimball / www.ronkimballstock.com; page 53 © Daniel Johnson; page 54 © Bob Langrish; page 55 © Dusty L. Perin; page 56, 57, 59, 60 © Bob Langrish; page 61 © Denver Bryan / denverbryan.com; page 63 © www.ronkimballstock.com; page 64 © Dusty L. Perin; page 65 © Bob Langrish; page 67 © Dusty L. Perin; page 68 © Denver Bryan / denverbryan.com; page 69 © Ron Kimball / www.ronkimballstock.com; page 70, 71 © Bob Langrish; page 73 © www.ronkimballstock.com; page 74, 75 © Denver Bryan / denverbryan.com; page 76 © Norvia Behling; page 77, 79 © Dusty L. Perin; page 80 © Denver Bryan / denverbryan.com; page 81 © Dusty L. Perin; page 83 © Bob Langrish; page 84, 85, 87, 88, 89 © Dusty L. Perin; page 91, 92 © Denver Bryan / denverbryan.com; page 93 © Dusty L. Perin; page 94 © Denver Bryan / denverbryan.com; page 95 © Norvia Behling; page 96 © Daniel Johnson

HORSE RULES

VIRTUES OF THE EQUINE CHARACTER

WILLOW CREEK PRESS

Companions

*Animals are such agreeable friends — they ask
no questions, they pass no criticism.*

GEORGE ELIOT

A true friend knows your weaknesses but shows you your strengths; feels your fears but fortifies your faith; sees your anxieties but frees your spirit; recognizes your disabilities but emphasizes your possibilities.

WILLIAM ARTHUR WARD

Little friends may prove great friends.

AESOP

*Our perfect
companions
never have fewer
than four feet.*

COLETTE

Companionship with animals is the most precious aloneness there is.

MARY BOSANQUET

Affectionate

Our sweetest experiences of affection are meant to point us to that realm which is the real and endless home of the heart.

HENRY WARD BEECHER

No act of kindness, no matter how small, is ever wasted.

AESOP

12

Our happiness in this world depends on the affections we are able to inspire.

DUCHESS PRAZLIN

We are shaped and fashioned by what we love.

JOHANN
WOLFGANG VON
GEOTHE

To love someone deeply gives you strength. Being loved by someone deeply gives you courage.

LAO TZU

Strong

Nature loves a burst of energy.

BOE LIGHTMAN

The horse weighs one thousand pounds and I weigh ninety-five. I guess I'd better get him to cooperate.

JOCKEY STEVE CAUTHEN

Commitment

*It seems essential, in relationships and all tasks,
that we concentrate only on what is most
significant and important.*

SOREN KIERKEGAARD

The achievement of your goal is assured the moment you commit yourself to it.

GEN. GEORGE S. PATTON

A total commitment is paramount to reaching the ultimate in performance.

TOM FLORES

Determination

*Nothing in the world can take the
place of persistence... Persistence and
determination are omnipotent.*

ATTRIBUTED TO CALVIN COOLIDGE

Knowledge is gained by learning; trust by doubt; skill by practice.

THOMAS SZASZ

He is able
who thinks
he is able.

BUDDHA

Desire

Clear your mind of can't.

SAMUEL JOHNSON

The starting point of all achievement is desire.

NAPOLEON HILL

Live that thou mayest desire to live again.

FRIEDRICH WILHELM NIETZSHE

Friendly

*A friend is somebody you want to be around
when you feel like being by yourself.*

BARBARA BURROW

Always hold your head up, but be careful to keep your nose at a friendly level.

MAX L. FORMAN

Those who bring sunshine to the lives of others cannot keep it from themselves.

JAMES BARRIE

The greatest sweetener in life is friendship.

JOSEPH ADDISON

He deserves paradise who makes his companions laugh.

THE KORAN

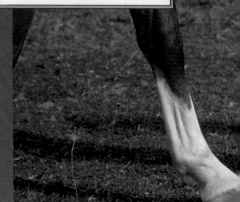

Gentleness

*Nothing is so strong as gentleness and nothing
is so gentle as real strength.*

RALPH W. SOCKMAN

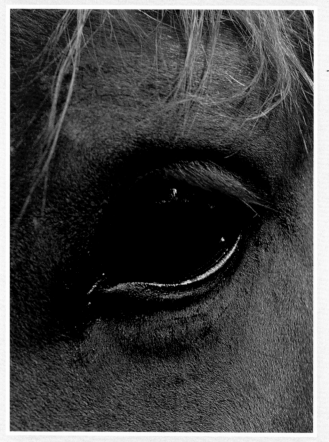

It is hard for the face to conceal the thoughts of the heart — the true character of the soul. — The look without is an index of what is within.

WILLIAM
SHAKESPEARE

40

Tenderness and kindness are not signs of weakness and despair, but manifestations of strength and resolutions.

KAHLIL GIBRAN

I learned that it is the weak who are cruel, and that gentleness is to be expected only from the strong.

LEO ROSTEN

Beautiful

*Whatever is in any way beautiful hath its source of
beauty in itself, and is complete in itself.*

MARCUS AUERLIUS ANTONIUS

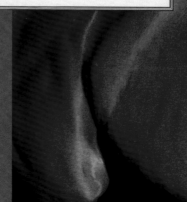

Consider this, the beauty and poetry of a horse in motion,
drawing its power from the ground into the very air
through which it moves, like Pegasus reborn.

MARGOT PAGE

Intelligent

There is just as much horse sense in the world as ever, but the horses have most of it.

ROBERT HEINLEIN

In partnership with a horse, one is seldom lacking for thought, emotion, and inspiration.

CHARLES DE KUNFFY

50

Horse sense is the thing a horse has which keeps it from betting on people.

W.C. FIELDS

Accomplished

*Everyone enjoys doing the kind of work
for which he is best suited.*

NAPOLEON HILL

Happiness...it lies in the joy of achievement.

FRANKLIN DELANO
ROOSEVELT

The highest of distinctions is service to others.

KING GEORGE VI

The secret of joy in work is contained in one word — excellence. To know how to do something well is to enjoy it.

PEARL S. BUCK

Success is the sum of small efforts — repeated day in and day out.

ROBERT COLLIER

Potential

Joy comes from using your potential.

WILL SCHULTZ

Let him who would enjoy a good future waste none of his present.

ROGER BABSON

Great ability develops and reveals itself increasingly with every new assignment.

BALTHASAR GRACIAN

61

Curious

*The larger the island of knowledge, the longer
the shoreline of wonder.*

Ralph W. Sockman

*A sense of
curiosity is
nature's original
school of
education.*

SMILEY
BLANTON

Curiosity can be vivid and wholesome only in proportion as the mind is contented and happy.

ANATOLE FRANCE

Playful

Not life, but good life, is to be chiefly valued.

SOCRATES

The time you enjoy wasting is not wasted time.

BERTRAND RUSSELL

Against the assault of laughter nothing can stand.

MARK TWAIN

Joyful

Did you ever see an unhappy horse? Did you ever see a bird that had the blues? One reason why birds and horses are not unhappy is because they are not trying to impress other birds and horses.

DALE CARNEGIE

*Good humor is one of the best articles of dress
one can wear in society.*

WILLIAM MAKEPEACE THACKERAY

All who would win joy, must share it;
happiness was born a twin.

LORD BYRON

We know nothing of tomorrow; our business is to be good and happy today.

SYDNEY SMITH

Loyal

Animals are reliable, many full of love, true in their affections, predictable in their actions, grateful and loyal. Difficult standards for people to live up to.

ALFRED A. MONTAPERT

Friend, our
closeness is this:
anywhere you
put your foot,
feel me in
the firmness
under you.

RUMI

*The best things in life are never rationed. Friendship,
loyalty, love, do not require coupons.*

G.T. HEWITT

Trusting

The best proof of love is trust.

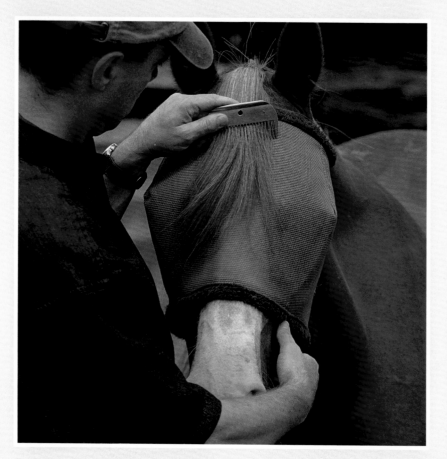

You may be deceived if you trust too much, but you will live in torment if you don't trust enough.

FRANK CRANE

Patient

Patience is the key to contentment.

MOHAMMED

Patience is the companion of wisdom.

SAINT
AUGUSTINE

The greatest power is often simple patience.

E. Joseph Cossman

Contented

He who does not care for Heaven but is
contented where he is, is already in Heaven.

H.P. BLAVATSKY

We never reflect how pleasant it is to ask for nothing.

SENECA

You can destroy your now worrying about tomorrow.

JANIS JOPLIN

Rest is not idleness, and to lie sometimes on the grass on a summer day listening to the murmur of water, or watching the clouds float across the sky, is hardly a waste of time.

Sir J. Lubbock

*The art of being happy lies in the power of extracting
happiness from common things.*

HENRY WARD BEECHER

Do not wish to be anything but what you are, and try to be that perfectly.

St. Francis de Sales